WE'RE ON YOUR SIDE, CHARLIE BROWN

Selected Cartoons from BUT WE LOVE YOU,
CHARLIE BROWN. Vol. 1

Charles M. Schulz

CORONET BOOKS
HODDER FAWCETT LTD.

Printed and bound in Great Britain for
Hodder Fawcett Ltd,
St. Paul's House, Warwick Lane,
London, E.C.4
by Hazell Watson & Viney Ltd,
Aylesbury, Bucks

ISBN 0 340 10760 X

RATS! A REAL VULTURE WOULD NEVER LET HIMSELF BE STARED DOWN!

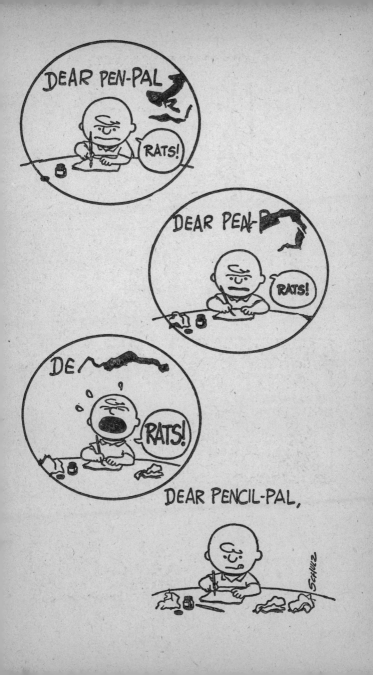

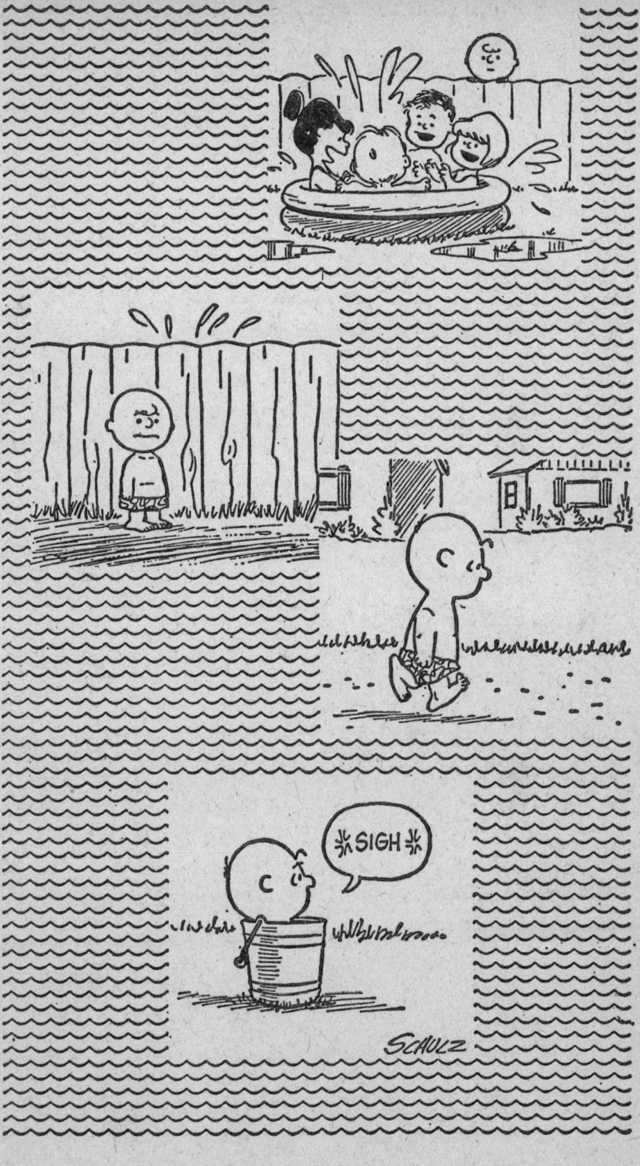

SIGH
SCHULZ